THE BUTCHART GARDENS

A FLOURISHING ESTATE

The BUTCHART GARDENS

A Flourishing Estate

#17, 1610 Derwent Way
Delta, B.C.
Canada V3M 6W1
Phone: (604) 521-1579
E-mail: brianj@naturalcolor.com
Website: www.naturalcolor.com

Photography by Bob Herger
Photography pages 11, 12, 19, 27, 34, 36, 37, 38, 43, 46, 51 by
Mickey Hayashi
Historical Photos supplied by City of Victoria Archives
Written by Marie Luttrell
Edited by Diane Johnston
Photo Editing by Brad Nickason
Design by Nickason Illustration and Design

Printed and bound in Singapore

CANADA CATALOGING
IN PUBLICATION DATA

ISBN 1-895155-15-0
. . . .

Cover: *Tulips announce the arrival of spring in
        The Sunken Garden.*
Following Pages: *Spring finery in The Sunken Garden.*

CONTENTS

A Flourishing Estate

6

"Benvenuto" Means Welcome

14

A Glimpse of Japan

34

Roses and Concerts

40

The Sunken Garden

48

A Heritage of Grace
and Beauty

62

A FLOURISHING ESTATE

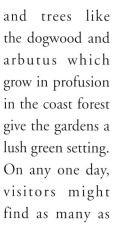

Nestled at the feet of the tall cedars and firs of a West Coast family estate, lie The Butchart Gardens, fifty acres of year-round floral delight. What was once a limestone quarry, with its eerie, lifeless landscape, has become a world-renowned landmark. The profusion of flowering plants, shrubbery and trees are set out in different areas, like the Sunken Garden, where the quarry once lay, the Italian Garden, the Victorian Rose Garden or the Japanese Garden. Throughout the many walkways, one can spot distinctive touches - statues, fountains, waterways - all woven into the aura of elegance and charm.

Flowers with such common appeal as zinnias and daisies, snapdragons and petunias intermingle with more exotic plants such as a handkerchief tree or the Tibetan blue poppy. Shrubbery like rhododendrons and azaleas, and trees like the dogwood and arbutus which grow in profusion in the coast forest give the gardens a lush green setting. On any one day, visitors might find as many as 300,000 plants in bloom. With so many blossoms, a stroll through The Butchart Gardens is not only a feast for the eyes, but enticingly fragrant. As well, the utter peacefulness of the forest setting is only disturbed by sounds of bird song, or bees visiting flowers. One might come upon gardeners at work changing over the plantings in one area, or hear the quiet chatter of visitors in a different language.

Above: The sign at the entrance to The Butchart Gardens gives an inkling of the enjoyment to come.
Right: Combining the exotic with the commonplace, the imported with indigenous, The Butchart Gardens display earns its world-renown.

Three quarters of a million visitors every year take the short drive from Victoria, British Columbia, (the major city on Vancouver Island and capital of British Columbia), to spend a peaceful day or evening at The Gardens. The guest book might offer names of callers from Germany, Taipei, New York, or Australia, and feature comments like, "Splendid", "Gorgeous", or "Breathtaking". The Butchart family still operates The Gardens with the same friendliness and welcome displayed by Jenny and Robert Pim Butchart as their original gardens attracted attention in the early 1900's. The Butcharts had offered tea, and benches, to their guests. Now visitors will find amenities such as two restaurants, a plant identification center, and a gift shop. Guide sheets are printed in 18 languages, wheelchairs are available so everyone can take in the extensive grounds. With The Gardens open every day from 9 am, visitors can see the early morning droplets of dew still fresh on the petals of a rose. They might see the full after-noon grandeur of the sun summoning the finest colours from the well- tended flower beds, or enjoy a peaceful evening stroll along romantically lit paths. Come with us, then, as we take you on a pictorial tour of the world famous Butchart Gardens.

Left: *A lovely brick walkway guides visitors through a profusion of springtime flowers like tulips and rhododendron. Spring blossoms begin in late February.*
Above: *Our Provincial flower, the Pacific Dogwood is especially beautiful in spring.*

Above: The coastal forest setting of The Butchart Gardens gives it an unusual charisma. Here, the sunlight captures the many shades of cineraria.

Right: Early morning watering leaves the walkway through the rose garden glistening. The Gazing Ball, a common feature in many Victorian gardens, flanked by stone benches, is set in the midst of hundreds of varieties of roses highlighted by tall delphiniums.

THE ROSE, A GIFT OF FRIENDSHIP

For gardeners the world around, the rose holds special significance as a flower of unique constancy, variety and beauty. It is widely recognized as the flower of love and romance.

The Butchart Gardens holds as its symbol a single red rose. Ninety years ago, Jenny Butchart received a gift of a single rose bush from a friend and fell in love with the art of gardening, beginning a whole new life for her family. The Butcharts honored the rose with its own area, the formal Rose Garden in keeping with their tradition of hospitality and friendship. It was designed in 1929 by Butler S. Sturtevant, a Seattle landscape architect. Each year, over 200 varieties of floribunda and tea roses are grown, and 80 varieties of climbing roses. Included in this vast array are "All-American" award winners, which were developed in many different countries.

July 1st is the peak of the season, and approximately 6600 blossoms with names like Apricot Nectar, Iceberg, Nicole, Butterscotch, American Pillar, or Can-Can scent the air with their heavenly fragrance.

Right: A profusion of snapdragons, a personal favorite of Mrs. Butchart, guides the way to the summerhouse. As part of the private garden, the summerhouse, just beyond a breezy archway covered in climbing roses, provided a place of refreshment for the Butchart family and friends.

Left: Hanging baskets can be found everywhere at The Butchart Gardens, to supplement ground displays or to accent the clean lines of a structure. Here a basket of geraniums revels in an early morning shower near the concert lawn.

"BENVENUTO" MEANS WELCOME

Benvenuto, the Italian word that means "welcome" was the name chosen by the Butcharts for their home. The original residence remains the heart from which flows the 50 acre garden site. No expense was spared in the building and expansion of their home, which the Butcharts acquired after their two daughters were grown. It featured such rooms as a billiard room, which also held a unique violin-piano, a treasure which Mr. Butchart found at a trade fair in Leipzig in 1928. A salt water swimming pool and even a bowling alley were part of the spacious home, and each room featured some type of floral display. The Butcharts were well known for their warmth and hospitality, as they hosted many guests. The extensive home, with its characteristic green roof, now houses the Dining Room Restauant, where one can be pampered with an elegant meal, the Plant Identification Center, offices and private family areas. Even the walls of the home are alive with Boston ivy, which turns a flaming red in the fall.

Adjacent to the house, greeting visitors when they arrive, are the information center, a coffee bar and gift shop, and the Blue Poppy Restaurant, where one can have a more casual meal, amid a full conservatory of flowers. Connecting the gift shop and restaurant is the Show Greenhouse, which overflows with exotic plants, that include its feature collection of many oversized begonias.

Above: Dahlias, a perennial favorite at The Butchart Grdens, are found in almost every colour but blue. It was named after Andreas Dahl a Swedish botanist

Right: The private gardens behind and to the west of "Benvenuto", the Butchart home.

At the back of the house, lays the formal Italian Garden. Once a tennis court, the centerpiece of the garden is a pond in the shape of a Florentine Cross, bedecked in water lilies. Surrounding the pond are raised flowerbeds, where one might find a selection of annuals such as the pink verbena which Jenny Butchart originally planted in the beds. Nearby, to complete the Italian ambience, a statue of Mercury keeps a watchful eye over the garden, surrounded by beds of impatiens, begonias, or chrysanthemums.

As one strolls farther from the house, amid the native greenery of cedar and rhododendron, one comes upon the star pond. The twelve-pointed star edged with a carefully clipped boxwood hedge, is fed by spouting frogs in the midst of a circular center bed of marsh marigolds. Surrounding the star pond is a larger circular bed teeming with tulips or begonias and heliotrope, depending on the time of year. People are welcome to stop and take in the beauty and atmosphere of each garden as they pass through. Because the gardens are stewarded with the vision of Jenny and Robert Butchart, as private and not botanical gardens, flowers and plants are not identified in their locations. Rather, the family encourages people to enjoy the whole effect, and will provide information about their plant life through the Plant Identification Center as well as through many informative guide brochures.

Left: The conservatory, built in 1930, now houses the Blue Poppy Restaurant, where patrons dine amid a wide variety of tropical plants which are grown year-round.

Above: "The Ring of Doves", added to The Butchart Gardens' fine collection of statuary in 1994, is set off by a bed of tulips and daffodils near the Begonia Bower.

Left: At the information center, walking guides for the
gardens are available in 18 languages.
Above: "Tacca" the boar, who stands watch in front of the
main house, delights visitors of all ages.

Left: Pots and hanging planters bring color to every part of The Gardens.
Here they compliment the geranium beds in front of the gift store.
Above: A side view of the main residence, with its ivy-covered walls and
trellised private garden, is seen through the unrestrained colours of snapdragons.

In the very early years of Butchart Gardens, curiosity seekers would be greeted at Benvenuto, the Butchart Estate, with a warm welcome and a cup of tea. Soon, it became a matter of course, and as the numbers increased, so did the popularity of the afternoon tradition. In 1915 alone, the family records show more than 18,000 cups of tea served, and often Jenny Butchart herself would be the one to pour. She was well known for her sense of fun and would sometimes go out into the gardens to invite total strangers to stay for dinner.

Today, meals are served in the Blue Poppy Restaurant, named for the Tibetan Blue Poppy which has grown into legend at The Gardens. Mrs. Butchart had acquired seed for it from the Edinburgh Botanical Garden soon after its discovery in 1920 by Captain F.M. Bailey, a British Army officer. In the more formal Dining Room Restaurant, one can be served a proper British tea daily, for which the whole Victoria area is known.

Left: Left: A baroque style cherub adds a whimsical touch to a pelargonium-ringed pond in the private gardens.
Above: The summer house, overlooking the private gardens,was a fine spot for the Butcharts to enjoy afternoon tea.

Above: Several species of water lilies are cultivated
in the ponds and fountains.
Right: The luxurious profusion of
annuals in the Italian Garden include golden zinnias,
verbena, cineraria, coreopsis and salvia.

Left: The mermaid and fish fountain is the focal point in the Italian
Garden, which was made in the shape of a Florentine cross.
Above: Symmetry even in the water lilies provides some of the attraction in the Italian
Garden, as well as a variety of plantings over the year. This exuberant "Ellen Wilmott"
variety of pink verbena is replaced in fall with white and yellow chrysanthemums.

Left: One of fifty gardeners stops to keep the
flower beds in exquisite condition.
Above: Collecting statues to suit each little niche had
been a lifelong pursuit of the Butcharts and the
Ross family has followed in their footsteps.

BEHIND THE SCENES

You might not see them on a visit to The Butchart Gardens, but you know they are there. Their careful work gives them away. It is not a troupe of elves who tend the flower beds, but a team of 50 gardeners. Over the years, ten head gardeners have directed the meticulous work .

During the course of the year, they work with the soil, the cycle of nature and, of course, the great variety of flowers and plants. Bedding plants are started in one of nineteen greenhouses, on site, and then they are set out in nurseries in another area of the estate until they are ready for their planting in the gardens about three months later. Three to four times in the year, the gardeners transform the beds throughout the fifty acres with a new crop of flowers and a new season begins. Approximately 400 other employees are involved in the operations of The Butchart Gardens, ranging from office personnel to kitchen workers, from entertainers to information staff. All employees are friendly and polite, and do their best to make a visit to the Gardens a special event.

. . . .

Left: The twelve-pointed star pond, at the North end of
the Italian Garden, is edged with boxwood and
surrounded with a circular bed of begonias and heliotrope.
Above: A stunning pink dahlia. Dahlias dazzle the eye
with their tall blossoms in shades like crimson, yellow,
orange and white, and are seen extensively from mid
summer to first frost.

Right: From the house and adjacent Italian Gardens, one can see past the Japanese Garden to Butchart Cove, part of Tod Inlet. A dock remains there, where Robert Butchart moored his yacht, to welcome visitors by sea.

Far right: Tulips embrace the warm spring sunshine. The Butchart Gardens augments their marvelous spring displays each year with 50,000 imported Dutch bulbs. Tulips were originally named from the Turkish word "tul-ban" meaning "turban" - a reference to the shape of the flower, and over 800 varieties are commonly grown.

A GLIMPSE OF JAPAN

Much like the Torii of Japan marking the entrance to a shrine area, the Torii gate at the entrance of the Japanese Garden marks the entrance to a different sort of garden. Here, the elements of water, tree, shrub even rock are carefully planned to give the visitor a new experience with each turn.

The earliest of all the areas in The Butchart Gardens to be developed, the Japanese Garden was designed by Isaboro Kishida soon after the Butcharts arrived at their beloved Benvenuto. It lies between the main house and the salt water of Tod Inlet. Permanent trees and shrubs are the focal points in the layout of the garden, with some trees delicately pruned to form balls of greenery. Cutleaf and Japanese maples provide welcome shade in the summer and brilliant foliage in the fall. Two weeping hemlock trees can be easily identified with their exotically hunched limbs. A small stream curls and then tumbles throughout the Japanese Garden, crossed by an arched wooden bridge. A stone lantern and a pair of bronze cranes help to add to the authentic Japanese atmosphere. Serenity through austerity, balance yet asymmetry are the effects which a Japanese garden might try to achieve. The garden serves as a microcosm of the natural world, where a rock might symbolize a mountain, or raked sand might represent water. Each season is as important as the next, so the guest might have a new experience of nature with each visit. A reflective walk through these Japanese gardens soothes the soul.

. . . .

Above: *The splendor of a delicate plum blossom in mid-spring.*

Right: *Stepping stones lead to a Japanese tea house in a tranquil scene of iris, fern, maple and cedar.*

. . . .

Left: An arched bridge takes visitors over a gentle stream. Japanese features such as the interplay of water, the careful pruning of trees and the stone lantern lend an aura of grace.
Above: A sand garden, Zen-style, where the stones, and the raking of patterns in the sand are scrupulously arranged.

THE ARTISTRY OF MAN

"Tacca" the boar loves to have his nose rubbed, and thousands of visitors do just that to wish for luck. A bronze replica of the boar at the Straw Market in Florence, Italy, he is representative of the many kinds of sculpture and statuary to be found in the 50 acre gardens.

In the Japanese Garden, one finds well weathered stone lanterns. In the Sunken Garden, the "Little Girl", sculpted by Victoria artist Edward Apt lifts spirits skyward. A fanciful snail sprays water in a small pond near the entrance of The Gardens. The Rose Garden gazing ball, the frog fountains in the Star Pond, the three sturgeons swirling about each other, the watchful eye of Mercury over the Italian Garden - almost anywhere in The Butchart Garden, one can find the blending of the artistry of man with the artistry of nature. Like the Butcharts before them, Ian Ross, the Butchart's grandson and heir to the estate, and his wife Ann-Lee Ross, are avid travelers and often return with a new plant or sculpture to add to their collection in The Gardens.

Left: A rare snowfall accentuates the gracious curves and the utter serenity of the Japanese Garden.
Above: Sakura - cherry blossoms. Cherry blossoms so inspired the Butcharts that they imported 566 flowering cherry trees to line the drive to the entrance of their estate.

ROSES AND CONCERTS

When the Butcharts first planted their rose garden in 1930, one of their considerations must have been the breezes from the west which would waft the heavenly aroma right to their door. Today 2500 rose plants from tea roses to climbers raise their heads to the sky and scent the air with their sweet perfume. As with many formal Victorian gardens, one can find a mirrored gazing ball and a sundial on either side of the main path. Leaving the Rose Garden one comes upon the Fountain of the Three Sturgeons, a bronze statue obtained by Mr. and Mrs. Ian Ross on a trip to Italy. Ian Ross, the grandson of the Butcharts, inherited the gardens for his 21st birthday in 1939. When he returned from the war in 1945, The Gardens had fallen into disrepair and he and his wife, Ann-Lee, made it their life's work to restore and enhance their legacy. For the fiftieth anniverary, in 1954, they installed underground lighting throughout The Gardens, the largest undertaking of its kind at the time. In 1964, Ian Ross designed and built the Ross Fountain from ordinary hardware. The jets of water constantly change, and are colourfully lit at night. The areas beyond the Rose Garden and the Fountain of the Three Sturgeons are the beautiful lawns and viewing areas where crowds gather on a summer evening to listen to music, watch the stars blink on one by one, or take in a display of fireworks. Tucked behind the lawns, one can see the plant nurseries, where the seedlings are planted out after their start in the greenhouses.

- -

Above: A dew-kissed rose at the height of summer.
Right: The breathtaking Rose Garden, where 2500 rose plants form a rainbow of delicate blooms.

. . . .

Left: *Tall delphiniums offer a backdrop to the thousands of beautiful rose blossoms.*

Right: *The Fountain of the Three Sturgeons, brought from Italy by Mr. and Mrs. Ian Ross. White flowering hydrangea, achillea, scented-leaf geraniums and fibrous begonias are but a few of the flowers which highlight this fountain.*

EVENING CELEBRATIONS

Summer evenings in this region of Canada feature beautiful sunsets and lingering twilights. West Coast residents as well as travellers love to take advantage of the long evenings to enjoy the out doors. Ian Ross, grandson of the Butcharts, decided years ago to make an evening spent at The Butchart Gardens memorable for all guests. What was once the kitchen garden for the Butchart family has now been transformed into a concert stage and lawn for summer evening entertainment, by the "Butchart Gardeners" from June through September. People of all ages enjoy singing along.

On Saturday evenings in July and August, near the plant nursery area, skies are lit up with fantastic fireworks displays choreographed to music by Christopher Ross, a great-grandson of the Butcharts.

Christmas Time brings another kind of life to The Gardens as The Gardens come alive with thousands of twinkling lights and festive music. An evening walk through The Gardens in December has become part of the holiday tradition for Victoria residents and visitors alike.

Left: Extensive, meticulously groomed lawns help to retain the feel of a grand estate.
Above: A hardy climbing rose blossoms inside a Victorian lampstand in the Rose Garden. The Rose Garden features a series of archways over the path, covered with climbing varieties of roses.

Far Left: *The handiwork of Jenny Butchart, who was assisted by many of the workers from Robert Butchart's cement factory, has been handed down for ninety years.*

Left: *An intricate network of dewdrops floats like a jeweled necklace above a moisture-veiled rose.*

THE SUNKEN GARDEN

The summer sun glints through cedars and Japanese maple trees. To the right of the path is a small log hut, that was perhaps once a playhouse for Butchart grandchildren, and you feel as if this is a magical path, leading to a place of mystery. Suddenly, at your feet 50 feet below is a wonderland of exuberant colors, every color of the rainbow, which beckons the senses to come see the beauty, come smell the fragrance, come feel the peace. 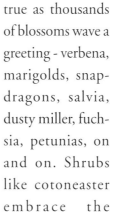 This garden is where the dream of Jenny Butchart began, and the shapes of flowerbeds, lawn, and ivy laden walls remain much as she had designed them over 90 years ago, with the assistance of landscape designer, W. J. Westby. A winding stairway leads to the floor of the former quarry, where a flagstone walkway wends its way through the vast floral array. It is a flower-lover's dream come true as thousands of blossoms wave a greeting - verbena, marigolds, snap-dragons, salvia, dusty miller, fuchsia, petunias, on and on. Shrubs like cotoneaster embrace the rock lookout in the center of the garden, with their fragrant blossoms attracting the attention of area bees. Ornamental maple and plum trees add the vivid red of their leaves to the splashes of color in the garden, while numerous evergreen shrubs and trees lend their deep green hues as rich background. Even the large arbutus tree with its peel-away red bark and glossy, leathery leaves stands watch over The Gardens.

Above: Nature's perfect shade of yellow.
Right: *The Sunken Garden, Jenny Butchart's triumphant legacy. Her vision, determination and hard work transformed what was once a limestone quarry into a paradise.*

At the far end of the quarry is The Sunken Garden lake, where the sculptured appearance of the Sunken Garden begins to soften into the natural feel of a West Coast wooded glen. Weeping willows stoop to touch the quiet lilied waters. Iris and plantain lilies enjoy the moist soil at water's edge, while rhododendrons and azaleas thrive in the shady glen. Pockets of plantings of begonias, heliotrope, and astilbe add visual and aromatic interest to the serenity of the walkway. 　　Finally, the path turns and overlooks the Ross Fountain, in another abandoned quarry. The rock walls have been left bare, and, except for the flower bed directly in front of the viewing area, the trees and plant life have rejuvenated themselves naturally. The contrast allows visitors to appreciate the beauty of the natural surroundings, in addition to the artistry of the master gardeners.

Above: The view point in the center of the Sunken Garden still wears the ivy coat which Jenny Butchart planted ninety years ago.
Right: Colors cascade down the walls of the quarry from the viewpoint to the flower beds below.

Left: A winding stairway leads guests from the lookout at the edge of the Sunken Garden to springtime delights.
Above: "The Little Girl" stands in a grotto on the west side of the Sunken Garden.

SHARING THE COLOURS

Jenny Butchart's dream of sharing their gardens with everyone grew by leaps and bounds. As more and more people visited, the requests for seeds led to the establishment of the "Benvenuto Seed Company" in 1920. By selling seeds, they were able to defray some of the enormous cost of upkeep of the gardens and until 1939, charged no one admission to the grounds.

As the fame of the Butcharts' green thumbs spread, so did the requests for cuttings and seeds. By 1920, the Butcharts established the "Benvenuto Seed Company".

From these beginnings, The Butchart Gardens developed its gift shop, located near the entrance and main residence. In a light and spacious setting, visitors can browse through mementos, gifts, ang gardening merchandise. Seed packets in an assortment of mixtures put together to the specifications of The Butchart Gardens, books and tools are available for the home gardener. Also, The Butchart Gardens produces its own mail order catalog.

. . . .

Left: *Nighttime illumination in the Sunken Garden, completed in 1954, was one of the earliest examples in North America of underground wiring and indirect lighting.*
Above: *The bold red and yellow tulips, and the dark green ivy of the quarry walls juxtaposed with a delicate ornamental plum tree and its globular clusters, provides a stunning visual contrast.*

Left: Built to commemorate the 60th anniversary of The Butchart Gardens, the Ross Fountain lies in a different quarried area from the Sunken Garden below a bed of spring blossoms.
Above: Fountains, like hidden treasures, can be found tucked exotically into small areas of The Gardens.

Above: No matter what time of year, nature displays an unrepeatable palette of hues. Here in
The Sunken Garden, these daffodils and annuals will be changed over in summer with
flowers like stocks, marigolds, chrysanthemums and verbena.
Right: Flowering trees can be found in every area of The Gardens. Whether in The Sunken Garden,
or in the Japanese or Rose Gardens, their sweet fragrance heightens the visitor's enjoyment.

. . . .

Left: Serenity is found at the Sunken Garden Lake.
*Above: An ore cart, once part of the booming cement
industry here, now serves as a planter.*

CEMENTING A START...

A lone smoke stack stands outside the Sunken Garden, one of the few reminders of the cement business which brought the Butcharts to Victoria at the turn of the 20th century.

Robert Pim Butchart had left his family hardware business in Ontario in the 1880's to establish himself in the business of manufacturing Portland cement. With the tremendous growth in cities, the demand for cement, not only for buildings, but for sidewalks and roads was skyrocketing. When Mr. Butchart discovered rich deposits of limestone at Tod Inlet, north of Victoria, he opened the Vancouver Portland Cement Company. An early innovation - packaging and shipping the cement in sacks rather than barrels - made a name for Mr. Butchart, and his company prospered.

Robert Butchart was a man of eclectic tastes. He collected art and instruments. He raised pigeons, and hand fed the trout in the Sunken Garden Lake. His love for his wife Jenny and her garden was readily evident in his warm welcome to the thousands of visitors. In 1928, Victoria awarded them the Freedom of the City, citing their "Public service and kindness of heart"

A Heritage of Grace and Beauty

In 1909, Jenny Butchart stood overlooking the limestone quarry near her home, "Benvenuto" on the Saanich Peninsula. Her husband, Robert Pim Butchart, had transferred a successful cement business here five years before, and now the quarry had been depleted of its rich limestone deposits. She wept as she gazed upon the eerie chasm. "Happily," she told a New York reporter years later,"the thought occurred - for which I shall ever thank God - to turn the unsightly spot in to a sunken garden."

With her husband fully in support of her, the boundless energy of Jenny Butchart took over and she orchestrated the monumental task. With the help of books, factory employees and acquaintances, tons of loam from a neighboring farm were carted in and the first of plentiful varieties of flowers, trees and shrubs were chosen and planted.

The Butcharts had always been adventuresome. Jenny had been a fine equestrienne in her youth and had tried her hand at flying soon after the world turned its eyes to airplane flight. Besides his success in business, Robert was one of the first people in British Columbia to own a car - license plate #14.

They tackled the project with gusto, moving quarry rock to form bases for raised flower beds and edging for other beds. Even the quarry walls were tended by Jenny's fine hand at planting, as she dangled over the side in a bos'un's chair

tucking ivy into every cranny.

Soon, more of the present gardens were developed. The Rose Garden was planted in 1930, with the Italian Garden replacing the estate's tennis court some time after. The Butcharts were avid world travelers, and never returned from a trip without a new variety of plant to add to their gardens.

Visitors were always welcome. Jenny's energy and charm were infectious as she greeted her guests or worked in the flowerbeds. Robert added a sign reading "Carve Initials Here" on one

tree, but refused any "Do Not" signs on the estate. To ease the bumpy ride from Victoria, the Butcharts supplied the cement for a mile-long road leading to Benvenuto, lined with 566 flowering cherry trees they had acquired in Japan.

When Robert's ill health forced them to move from their beloved "Benvenuto" in 1939, the estate was passed to Ian Ross, the son of their elder daughter, Jennie. While he completed his education at McGill University, and served a tour of military duty in World War II, the family solicitor, Mr. H. J. Davis oversaw the operations of The Gardens. Robert Butchart died in 1943 at the age of 87 and Jenny died in 1950, also in her eighties.

On his return, Ian and his wife Ann-Lee Ross worked tirelessly not only to restore The Gardens to their former beauty, but to expand and enhance the collections of flora, fountains and other attractions. To celebrate the 50th and 60th anniversaries of "Benvenuto", they added night illumination and the Ross Fountain, respectively. Evening entertainment was added to the draw of The Gardens themselves, as well as the addition in more recent years of fireworks, Christmas lights and carollers. In order to accomplish these feats, the number of employees has swelled to 450.

Even still, the hand of Jenny Butchart can be found in the care and welcome at the Butchart Gardens.

Like any work of art, The Butchart Gardens merits visiting again and again. Each time, one might notice something new. In spring, thousands of tulips and daffodils wave to the blossoming cherries and plums. Hanging baskets bring colorful appeal to the budding roses in the formal Rose Garden. Summer brings a change of clothes, with flower beds decked out in their finest hues. Some, like the cosmos reach high into the sky, while the lowly forget-me-nots lend their fragile beauty to the profusion of colorful blooms. The Tibetan blue poppy, one of the first rare species to be grown at The Gardens can be seen in bloom, steps from the Torii in the Japanese Garden. Flowers bear names like bears breeches, the obedient plant, candytuft, and firethorn. Visitors in the fall marvel at the late season blooms, such as hydrangeas, with their pom-pom blossoms ranging from white through pinks, through deep blues, still found through late October. Chrysanthemums, and polyanthus, boldly wear their colors through the crisp autumn days. The highlight of a fall visit, though, is the foliage, with flaming reds and oranges, bright yellows set against the evergreen forest. At Christmas time, a little human help lights up the gardens with thousands of lights, and beautiful carols. On a fine winter day, a peaceful walk through the grounds brings out the subtler side of the Gardens. One might find the early arrival of crocuses or snowdrops in January, or a colorful display of berries or rosehips. With the mild Coastal climate - snow is rare, and temperatures average about 38 degrees in January - the Victoria area enjoys an extended growing season. A yearly tradition is the February blossom count, and home gardeners tally blooms in the hundreds of thousands. The Butchart Gardens, 11 miles from Victoria, has used this mild climate to its advantage and opens every day of the year. Visitors never go away disappointed, finding in this garden wonderland, a glittering jewel of captivating delight.